First World War
and Army of Occupation
War Diary
France, Belgium and Germany

60 DIVISION
181 Infantry Brigade
London Regiment
2/22 Battalion
4 October 1915 - 31 December 1915

WO95/3032/4

The Naval & Military Press Ltd
www.nmarchive.com
Published in association with The National Archives

Published by

The Naval & Military Press Ltd

Unit 10 Ridgewood Industrial Park,

Uckfield, East Sussex,

TN22 5QE England

Tel: +44 (0) 1825 749494

www.naval-military-press.com

www.nmarchive.com

This diary has been reprinted in facsimile from the original. Any imperfections are inevitably reproduced and the quality may fall short of modern type and cartographic standards.

© Crown Copyright
Images reproduced by permission of The National Archives, London, England, 2015.

Contents

Document type	Place/Title	Date From	Date To
Heading	WO95/3032/4		
Heading	60 Division 181 Brigade 2/22 London Regt 1915 Oct-1915 Dec		
Miscellaneous	Statement to be Annexed to War Diary 2/22nd B'n London Regt (The Queen's)	04/09/1915	04/09/1915
War Diary	Hockerill Camp Bishops Stortford	04/10/1915	26/10/1915
War Diary	Hockerill Camp	01/11/1918	04/11/1913
War Diary	Dunmow	09/11/1918	13/11/1913
War Diary	Havers Lane	15/11/1918	15/11/1913
War Diary	Wagon Park	15/11/1918	15/11/1913
War Diary	Bishops Stortford	15/11/1918	15/11/1913
War Diary	Dunmow	17/11/1918	30/11/1913
Heading	War Diary of 2/22nd Battalion London Regiment From 1st December 1915-31st December 1915		
War Diary	Dunmow	01/12/1915	31/12/1915
Miscellaneous	Appendix "A"		
Miscellaneous	Appendix "B"		
Miscellaneous	Outpost Scheme of 2/22nd Battalion London Regiment Dunmow	31/12/1915	31/12/1915
Operation(al) Order(s)	Order No.1	31/12/1915	31/12/1915

WO 95/3032/4

60 Division

181 Brigade

2/22 London Regt

1915 Oct – 1915 Dec

2904

Statement to be annexed to War Diary
2/22nd B'n London Regt (The Queen's)

Brigade.	101st Infantry Brigade.
Division.	60th (London) Division.
Mobilization Centre.	
Temporary War Station.	Bermondsey.
Stations since occupied subsequent to Concentration.	White City, London. Redhill, Surrey. St Albans, Herts. Bishops Stortford, Herts. Hockerill Camp, Bishops Stortford, Herts.
Training.	The finding of Guards and Fatigues still seriously handicaps training generally. Musketry training with the .303 rifle has ceased altogether — training with the Japanese Rifle has been proceeded with but no range firing has been done. The fact that there is only one Machine Gun in the Brigade mitigates against successful training with this arm.
Supply Services.	Quite satisfactory.
Billeting	Nothing to add — the Battalion has now moved into camp.
Remounts.	Excellent.
Re-organisation of T.F. into Home and Imperial Service.	Nothing to add.
Preparation of Units for Imperial Service.	See remarks under Training.

Hockerill Camp
Bishops Stortford.
4th September 1915.

Theodore Brinckman
Colonel
Comdg 2/22nd Battalion London Regt.

Army Form C. 2118.

WAR DIARY
or
INTELLIGENCE SUMMARY

(Erase heading not required.)

2/22 LONDON

Instructions regarding War Diaries and Intelligence Summaries are contained in F. S. Regs., Part II. and the Staff Manual respectively. Title pages will be prepared in manuscript.

Hour, Date, Place	Summary of Events and Information	Remarks and references to Appendices
Hockerill Camp, Bishops Stortford. 4th October 1915.	N I L	Training during the month proceeded on Normal lines.

[signature] Col.
Comdg. 2/22nd Bn London Regiment

1247 W 3299 200,000 (E) 8/14 J.B.C. & A. Forms/C. 2118/11.

Army Form C. 2118.

WAR DIARY
or
INTELLIGENCE SUMMARY.

(Erase heading not required.)

For the Month of October 1915.

B

Hour, Date, Place	Summary of Events and Information	Remarks and references to Appendices
Hockerill Camp Bps Stortford. 5-8th October 1915.	3rd Army Manoeuvres	Apart from the manoeuvres mentioned, the training of the Battalion proceeded on Normal Lines.
19-22nd " 1915.	ditto.	
26th October 1915.	A draft of 3 N.C.Os and 44 men proceeded to join the 3/22nd B'n London Regiment, at Tadworth.	

Comdg. 2/22nd B'n London Regiment.

2/22 Bn. London Regiment. B.

Confidential

Army Form C. 2118

WAR DIARY
— or —
INTELLIGENCE SUMMARY
(Erase heading not required.)

Instructions regarding War Diaries and Intelligence Summaries are contained in F. S. Regs., Part II. and the Staff Manual respectively. Title Pages will be prepared in manuscript.

Place	Date 1915	Hour	Summary of Events and Information	Remarks and references to Appendices
HOCKERILL CAMP	Nov 1st	9 AM	A detachment of 100 N.C.O.s & men under Capt A. McCOMAS and 2/Lieut C.F. ALDRICH marched out & entrained for LITTLE EASTON, where they took over guard duties at 2nd Army Headquarters.	See WAR
HOCKERILL CAMP	Nov 4	9 AM	The Battalion (less above detachment) marched by route march to DUNMOW arriving there at 12.45 PM. During the afternoon the Battalion was put into close billets in 4 empty buildings near the town.	WAR
DUNMOW	Nov 9	9.30 AM	A detachment of 100 N.C.O.s & men under Capt. L.G. COLMER and 2/Lieut N.M. HAYFORD moved by route march to LITTLE EASTON to replace detachment above & find guard duties at 2nd Army Headquarters.	WAR
DUNMOW	Nov 13		525 .303 LEE ENFIELD (converted) rifles & 157,920 rounds .303 ammunition received and taken on charge of the Battalion.	WAR
HAVERS LANE WALLN. PARK. MANIS BISHOPS. STORTFD.	Nov 15	2.20 PM	8 civilian wagons exchanged for 8 G.S. wagons in accordance with Divisional letter 23/4/8 13/11/15	WAR
DUNMOW	Nov 17		Hon Major letter of Infantry 1 (Y.73) dated 8.11.15 adducing establishment of Officers & Territorial Force 2nd Line Infantry Battalions to 23, received.	WAR
DUNMOW	Nov 20		591 JAPANESE rifles and 106,445 rounds .256 (JAPANESE) ammunition dispatched to WEEDEN.	WAR
DUNMOW	Nov 21	2 PM	Inspection of Battalion Officers & civil vehicles occasionally by Col DAVIDSON-HOUSTON accompanied by the Commanding Officer of the Central Force.	WAR
DUNMOW	Nov 22		8 civil transport horses of the establishment and transferred to 1st Brigade R.F.A. STANSTEAD.	WAR
DUNMOW	Nov 30		15 officers transferred to the 3/22 Bn. London Regt at WEST CROYDON in accordance with instructions contained in War Office Letter of Infantry 1 (Y=3) dated 8.11.15.	See Appendix.

H.T. Griffe
Comdg. 2/22nd Bn London Regiment.

Confidential
War Diary of
2/22nd Battalion London Regiment
from 1st December 1915 – 31st December 1915.

Confidential

Army Form C. 2118

WAR DIARY
or
INTELLIGENCE SUMMARY
(Erase heading not required.)

Instructions regarding War Diaries and Intelligence Summaries are contained in F.S. Regs., Part II. and the Staff Manual respectively. Title Pages will be prepared in manuscript.

Place	Date	Hour	Summary of Events and Information	Remarks and references to Appendices
DUNMOW	Dec 1		Training much handicapped owing to heavy & continuous rain. WR	
DUNMOW	Dec 2	8 AM	Battalion marched out for Brigade exercise at ABBOTS HALL (1 mile South of SHALFORD) WR Weather fine, dry & warm.	
DUNMOW	Dec 3		Training much handicapped by continuous rain. 42,000 rounds .303 ammunition transferred to OC 2/7 LONDON Rifle Brigade Ammunition Column at STANSTEAD WR	
DUNMOW	Dec 4		Training much handicapped as equipment ammunition etc. Weather changeable WR	
DUNMOW	Dec 5		Col Sir THEODORE BRINCKMAN Bart C.B. having returned from sick leave resumed command	
DUNMOW	Dec 6		of the Battalion. All officers medically examined & passed fit for service overseas. Training much handicapped by rain. WR	
DUNMOW	Dec 7		Training proceeded on normal lines, the morning rain afternoon WR	
DUNMOW	Dec 8		Training proceeded on normal lines fine WR	
DUNMOW	Dec 9		Battn. marched out at 9AM for Battn. exercise in outpost duties the enemy being seen in afternoon. WR	
DUNMOW	Dec 10		Inspection of all .303 rifles on harness of Battn. by 131st (Infantry) Brigade Commander. Fine & dry with light wind. WR	
DUNMOW	Dec 11		Advance of DUNMOW town opposed by C Coy as Rebels, by Brigade Commander Col Sir WR	
DUNMOW	Dec 12		C.O.? the same WR	
DUNMOW	Dec 13		Training proceeded on normal lines. Very cold & fine WR	

1875 W: W593/826 1,000,000 4/15 J.B.C. & A. A.D.S.S./Forms/C. 2118.

WAR DIARY / INTELLIGENCE SUMMARY

Army Form C. 2118

(Erase heading not required.)

Instructions regarding War Diaries and Intelligence Summaries are contained in F. S. Regs., Part II. and the Staff Manual respectively. Title Pages will be prepared in manuscript.

Place	Date 1915	Hour	Summary of Events and Information	Remarks and references to Appendices
DUNMOW	Dec 14		Training much handicapped by snow. WR	
DUNMOW	Dec 15		Training much handicapped by snow. WR	
DUNMOW	Dec 16		Battalion marched out at 9 A.M. for route march under Battalion arrangements. Fine. WR	
DUNMOW	Dec 17		Battalion marched out at 9 A.M. for Battalion exercise in Aspects. Fine. WR	
DUNMOW	Dec 18		Training proceeded on normal lines. Fine. WR	
DUNMOW	Dec 19		Fine & cold	
DUNMOW	Dec 20		Training proceeded on normal lines but - Cold. WR	
DUNMOW	Dec 21		Brigade scheme under Battalion arrangement at 9 A.M. WR	
DUNMOW	Dec 22		Training much handicapped by snow. WR	Appendix A
DUNMOW	Dec 23		Inspection of the Battalion by Major General F. S. Ralph C.V.O. C.B. Commanding Co. (London) Division (TF) Number of Officers on parade 14. Men 261. Fine morning, Snow in the afternoon. WR	WR WR WR WR Train Appendix B
DUNMOW	Dec 24		Training proceeded on normal lines. Fine morning, Rain in the afternoon	
DUNMOW	Dec 25		Church Parade. Wet morning - fine afternoon	
DUNMOW	Dec 26		Church Parade. Dull	
DUNMOW	Dec 27		Holiday. Wet	
DUNMOW	Dec 28		Company training. Fine	
DUNMOW	Dec 29		Company & platoon training, weather fine	
DUNMOW	Dec 30		Battalion Route march. Weather fine. Time of parade 9.15 AM. Bn returned to billets 1.30 pm	
DUNMOW	Dec 31		The Battalion practised outpost scheme (scheme attached) but brought to a stand still by the weather	

Theodore Breereton
Col.
Comdg. 2/22nd Bn London Regiment

APPENDIX "A".

Notes with reference to strength of Battalion on G.O.C'S Inspection December 23rd 1915, by Captain & Adjutant A. MAYER, 2/22nd Battalion London Regiment.

The G.O.C. remarked on the small number of men on parade, Viz, 261, and it was explained to him that this was due to

(a) The large number of Officers & Men employed on extra regimental duties.

(b) The number of light duty men who have been recommended for discharge, but whose discharge has not been sanctioned by the War Office.
In support of this explanation the following figures were shown to the G.O.C.

N.C.O's & Men on Parade		261
Christmas Leave	60	
3rd Army Guard at Little Easton	100	
Rear Party at Bishops Stortford	22	
Courses	18	
Brigade & Divisional Orderlies	7	
Machine Gun Section Brigaded at Braintree	28	
Regtl. Employ including Guards	33	
Absent	8	
Hospital	14	
Detention	4	
Leave	2	
Sick	12	
Sick Leave	8	
Light Duty (unable to carry pack and rifle)	34	350
STRENGTH OF BATTALION		611

Officers on Parade		14
Officers on Special Leave	1	
" on Sick Leave	2	
3rd Army Guard, Little Easton	2	
Attached 3rd Army Headquarters	1	
In command of rear guard	1	
Instructing at Courses	1	
Attending Courses	1	
Acting Brigade Machine Gun Officer	1	10
		24

Appendix "B".

Tactical Exercise 31st December 1915

2/22nd Battalion London Regiment.

OPERATION ORDERS

by

Col. Sir Theodore Brickman Bart. C.B.,
Commanding.

APPENDIX "B".

Ref: 1" Ord. Survey.

OUTPOST SCHEME of 2/22ND BATTALION LONDON REGIMENT, DUNMOW, for FRIDAY 31st December 1915.

GENERAL IDEA.

A Force advancing on COLCHESTER is halted on the 31st instant at BISHOPS STORTFORD.

The G.O.C. has decided to hold the outpost line BROXTED-GT. CANFIELD. Enemy Scouts have been located at BRAINTREE.

SPECIAL IDEA.

DUNMOW.

31st December 1915.

The 2/22ND BATTALION LONDON REGIMENT will hold the Sector from BAMBER'S GREEN exclusive to FROGS HALL (400 yards due West of LITTLE CANFIELD HALL) inclusive.

ORDER NO. 1.

2/22ND BATTALION LONDON REGIMENT.

DUNMOW.

Ref: 1" Ord. Survey Sheet 98.　　　　　　　　　　　　31st December 1915.

　　　　　　　　　　　　The Battalion will march at 9 a.m. to occupy the sector as in the Special Idea.

Starting point.　　　　　2/22nd Battalion London Regiment Headquarters.

Major Thompson　　　　　"A" Coy will occupy the sector of the position from BAMBER'S GREEN to 300 yards S.S.E.

Capt. Carr-Gomm　　　　　"B" Coy from the right flank of "A" Coy to 300 yards S.

Capt. McComas　　　　　　"C" Coy from right flank of "B" Coy to 300 yards S.

Capt. Richardson　　　　"D" Coy from right flank of "C" Coy S to FROGS HALL inclusive.

Reports.　　　　　　　　Reports will be sent to FROGS HALL.

　　　　　　　　　　　　　　　　　　　　　　　　　　A. Mayes
　　　　　　　　　　　　　　　　　　　　　　　　CAPT. & ADJUTANT.
　　　　　　　　　　　　　　　　　　　　　　　　2/22 Bn London Regt

Issued at 8 a.m.

Dictated to O.C. "A" Coy
　　"　　 to O.C. "B"　"
　　"　　 to O.C. "C" 　"
　　"　　 to O.C. "D" 　"

Copy No. 1 retained for Operation Order File
　　"　　 2　　"　　　"　War Diary.

www.ingramcontent.com/pod-product-compliance
Lightning Source LLC
Chambersburg PA
CBHW081517160426
43193CB00014B/2713